HOW TO SURVIVE
& THRIVE
IN COLLEGE

From Buying Textbooks, Dealing With Weird
Roommates, Mastering Your Exams,
Handling Stress, Preparing for your Future
and Everything in Between

By
Pete Bennet

ISBN: 978-1-957590-31-8

For questions, email: Support@AwesomeReads.org

Please consider writing a review!

Just visit: AwesomeReads.org/review

FREE BONUS

SCAN TO GET OUR NEXT BOOK FOR FREE!

TABLE OF CONTENTS

INTRODUCTION:

HOW TO USE THIS BOOK

Whether you're eighteen years old and just about to leave the nest, starting your college career after a few years of working and traveling, or returning to school after a few years off, the next four years of your life are going to be some of the most exciting you've ever experienced. During your college years, you'll not only learn more about yourself, but you'll also learn how to get along with other people, discover your passions in life, and make connections that will last a lifetime.

As a college student, many of you will be setting out into the world on your own for the first time. No longer will you have your parents at home to cook your dinner, do your laundry, or tell you when to get out of bed. Now that you're a college student, this is all up to you—you're on your own! For the first time in your life, you'll be independent. This probably sounds like the freedom you've always been looking for, but it does come along with a lot more responsibility. On top of studying for your classes and maintaining your social life, you also need to make sure you do your own laundry, manage your time well, and make sure you're eating healthily to avoid the dreaded freshman fifteen.

Don't get us wrong — we're not trying to make college sound like a drag. Although your main job in college is to be a student and do your best to prepare yourself for the rest of your life, you'll also meet people who will become lifelong friends. You'll juggle living with a roommate in your dorm, going out on the weekends, and deciding whether it's more important to study on a weeknight or go get dinner with friends.

Although college is a great deal of fun and offers a plethora of new experiences, it's also a time in your life when you're going to be challenged. You'll take classes unlike anything you ever experienced in high school and will learn new tips and tricks in order to succeed in your studies. In fact, many new college students find they were able to get away with some poor study habits in high school, but when they get to college, those old habits don't work quite as well as they used to.

In this book, we cover everything you'll need to know to survive and thrive during your time in college. By reading and fully understanding the contents of this book, you'll know what to do to rock your college years, from your first welcome weekend to your senior year, and setting yourself up for success in the workforce. From creating the perfect study schedule to making sure you have enough time to spend with your friends, once you finish this book, you'll be ready to not only survive your college years but master them.

CHAPTER ONE:

THE SUMMER BEFORE COLLEGE

You've been accepted by the college of your dreams, you walked across the stage and threw your hat into the air at your high school graduation, and now it's the middle of summer, and you're getting ready to start the next four years of your life as a college student. You feel excited about the impending independence and freedom of your college life, and you also have this burning question in your mind—what do you do to prepare for your first year of college?

As a college student, you'll be challenged in a way that you've never experienced before. You'll take interesting classes to learn about your future career, find your passion in this world, and above all, you'll learn how to become an adult. This is likely the first time you've ever been on your own, and it's incredibly exciting! However, that independence also means there will be new responsibilities you must take on.

That said, one of the best ways to prepare for your first semester of college is to spend the summer transitioning. This means you'll need to take care of some important business, but make sure you have fun while you're doing it.

For those of you who are feeling a bit nervous about getting ready to go off to college, just know there's plenty of preparation you can do to help you feel more ready. Be prepared to dot your i's and cross your t's and make sure everything is arranged for you to be successful. This includes getting appointments out of the way, gathering your school materials, and reaching out to future roommates.

SCHEDULE APPOINTMENTS

Especially if you'll be going to school out of state, it's important to schedule all of your doctor and other health appointments before you leave. Although you can certainly find doctors and dentists while you're away at school, many students find it easier to schedule these appointments before they leave for college.

Many colleges have a nurse or nurse practitioner on site to see students for minor illnesses. However, they don't often do general checkups or specialty medical procedures. So, make sure to see your eye doctor and your dentist and get all your prescriptions filled before you leave.

In addition, many colleges require you to have some sort of vaccination record and required vaccines. Make sure to check your school's requirements and get those documents sent to your school before your first day. If you're unsure of where to find these documents, you can reach out to your school's student resource offices or any other person you have been corresponding with at your college.

EXPLORE

Your college campus is not the only place where you'll be spending time when you go off to college. In fact, you should get to know the entire town surrounding your college. One of the biggest mistakes that new college students make is not exploring the town around them when they get to college. Although there are many opportunities, activities, and events on campus, there's nothing like getting out into the community and learning what it has to offer you as well.

Part of exploring your new town is getting to know where the local stores are as well as where you can purchase the things you need. You should become familiar with local drugstores for your prescriptions, the nearest grocery store for your food needs, and, importantly, the closest (and best) place to find a late-night pizza!

CONNECT WITH
YOUR ROOMMATE

You'll likely be paired with your roommate at the end of your senior year or at some point over the summer. It's a great idea to reach out to your roommate during the summer so you two can meet, either in person or remotely. Because you'll be living with your roommate or roommates, it's important to get to know them. Some of the things you should consider asking your roommate include:

- What they like to do
- What their major is or what their interests are
- If they are a morning person or a night person
- If they like to go out or stay in
- If they have any allergies
- If they are cleaner or messier
- What their pet peeves are
- The best way to communicate with each other

Oftentimes, colleges have you fill out a questionnaire so they can match you with a roommate who has a similar personality or similar habits as you. Typically, colleges do their best to pair the more social people together and pair the homebodies together. In addition, they often place college athletes together and try to pair people who have similar hygiene habits (aka, they put those who really care about organization together and pair those who are more relaxed with their living space together).

If your college doesn't send you a questionnaire to fill out for them to pair you with a roommate, there's no need to worry. You'll get to meet a lot of different people and will learn how to get along with those around you. If you do ever find yourself dealing with some roommate drama, don't fret! We will cover how to deal with roommate conflict later in this book.

GATHER SCHOOL MATERIALS

To be the most prepared for your first week of college, gather all the school materials you will need to be successful. This may involve buying a new planner, a new set of notebooks, new headphones, or even updating your laptop or tablet. Most importantly, you should make sure you have school materials that help you remain organized and make you excited to learn.

Because not everyone has the money to buy all new school materials, you should check out your school scholarship opportunities to see if they have funds for getting new electronics. You can also take out extra loan money to pay for school expenses such as school materials and textbooks. We'll cover this in more detail in the next chapter.

BUY YOUR
TEXTBOOKS

The next step to being prepared for your freshman year is to make sure you have all of your textbooks. If you register for your classes before your first week, you should receive a list of textbooks from the professor of the class. If the professor doesn't email the required list of textbooks, you can often find them on your student portal or online.

Some schools will have you register for classes during your orientation week, so if you don't have the option to buy textbooks yet, this isn't something you need to worry about immediately. In addition, many textbooks are now available online, so if you're worried about having your books on time, you can always get the electronic versions and download them immediately. The bookstore at your school also almost always has the textbooks you need, and you can buy them in person once you figure out your textbook list.

DECORATE
YOUR DORM ROOM

Designing your dorm room is one of the most exciting parts of getting started at college. If you don't already have a Pinterest board to help you design the lights, create your ultimate gaming center, and dream about the comfy beanbag chairs you want in your dorm room, now's your chance.

There are many places where you can buy dorm decorations and get everything you need for college. Just check out your favorite home goods stores and see what they have to offer. Most of the time, you can find a college checklist available either online at these stores or even as a paper copy in the store. Some of the common items that should be on your dorm room checklist include:

- Comforter, sheets, pillows, blankets
- Mattress pads — mattresses provided by colleges are notoriously uncomfortable
- Alarm clock
- Towels
- Bath caddy
- Flip-flips for showering — avoid nasty foot fungus!
- Storage for under your bed
- Laundry baskets
- Posters
- Lights
- Adhesive hooks for hanging
- Bed risers
- Floor lamp
- Desk lamp

- Desk chair
- Additional seating for your guests—check out bean bags, futons, or poufs
- Bulletin board
- Dry erase board
- Closet organizers
- Rugs—especially if you have concrete or tile floors
- Curtains

Although you don't have to, it can be a fun bonding experience to design your dorm room with your future roommate. The two of you can coordinate colors and even split the cost of the items that you'll both use, such as guest seating, rugs, curtains, and door decorations.

CREATE A BUDGET

College is expensive; there's no hiding it. Make sure you create a realistic college budget, so you don't spend your entire high school savings in one year. Luckily, your freshman year is typically covered by your loans because most colleges require you to live on campus and have a meal plan your first year. Regardless, make sure you budget for:

- Gas

- Car payments
- Snacks and food
- Clothes
- School materials
- Personal hygiene items
- Spending money for restaurants and activities

SET YOUR MOVING DATE

Typically, freshmen move into dorms during welcome week or orientation, but the move-in dates often span the course of a weekend. That said, you should figure out when you want to officially move into your dorm. There are definitely some advantages to moving in earlier, such as having your choice of bed in the dorm room, taking a shower before the masses arrive, getting a jump start on decorating the room, and having more time to settle in before the festivities begin. But if you do arrive later, that's no problem at all — you'll still have plenty of time to get settled before classes begin.

If you're a student athlete who plays a fall sport, you may even have the opportunity to move in much earlier. Practices often start well before the beginning of the semester, so athletes can often move in up to a month before the rest of the freshman cohort.

SPEND TIME WITH FAMILY AND FRIENDS

Your last task of the summer is to spend time with friends, family, and your significant other, if you have one. Going off to college is not goodbye forever, but you'll likely not see your high school friends and family nearly as often as you're used to. So make sure to spend the summer soaking up time with your loved ones!

CHAPTER TWO:

WAYS TO PAY FOR COLLEGE

College is expensive, but it's important because it's an investment in your future. Luckily, there are several ways that you can pay for college. From student loans to applying for scholarships, this chapter will help you find a way to pay for your education.

WHAT DO LOANS COVER IN COLLEGE

Contrary to popular belief, loans cover more than just college tuition. In fact, you can use loans to cover your living expenses. This means that your loans can cover:

- Tuition and fees
- Books and supplies
- Room and board, aka rent and food
- Transportation
- Personal expenses

While loans will cover everything you need to be comfortable, you can only take out the amount that your college determines covers the cost of attendance. This amount will vary depending on where your campus is located and the average cost of living in that area, so you'll have to check your college's financial aid website to determine how much you can take out to cover living expenses.

HOW TO PAY
FOR COLLEGE

Although many people think about loans when they think about paying for college, there are many other options for you to consider to help you pay for your college degree. In fact, loans are truly just the beginning when it comes to the various ways that you can pay for college. Yet it's important to understand all your options, so you don't find yourself in over your head when it comes to debt or finding ways to pay your tuition.

FEDERAL
GRANTS

A federal grant is free financial aid that comes from the US Department of Education. They are typically awarded to students and their families based on identified financial need.

Federal grants do not need to be repaid, so they are one of the best ways to pay for college if you qualify.

If you want to see if you qualify for a federal grant, you'll have to submit the Free Application for Student Aid, commonly known as the FAFSA. You will need to submit the FAFSA each year you plan on attending college. It won't hurt to fill out the form, and if you can qualify for some federal grants, that will be a big step toward paying for college.

WORK STUDY

Work-study is a federal program that you may be awarded as part of your financial aid package. Work-study is essentially part-time work that will allow you to make money to pay for your education. If you qualify for a work-study program, you can work on campus and will even likely have the pick of jobs on campus. In fact, many colleges will award on-campus jobs to students in work-study programs before they are offered to students who did not qualify for work-study.

COLLEGE SAVINGS ACCOUNT

Some students have the privilege of owning or having access to a college savings account. You or your parents can make tax-free contributions to a college savings account that can be used to cover educational expenses, including your tuition, fees, room and board, books, and other living expenses. Talk to your parents if you're unsure whether you have a college savings account because this can help you pay for a significant portion of your education.

LOANS

One of the most common ways to pay for your degree is by taking out student loans. This should be the last option you use to pay for college because you'll need to pay these loans back. Both federal and private loans are available to college students, but make sure to be aware of the interest rates of the loans you're considering because sometimes private loans have significantly higher interest rates than federal loans.

When you get your FAFSA information back, it will include the types of loans you can take out for that year. The two common types of federal loans that you'll likely be offered are subsidized and unsubsidized loans. A subsidized loan does not accrue interest while you're still in school, but an unsubsidized loan will accrue interest as you go through school. That said, subsidized loans should be the loans that you accept first.

SCHOLARSHIPS

Scholarships are similar to grants because you do not have to repay them. Instead of being based on financial need, scholarships are often based on other factors such as academics, sports, competitions, and more.

One of the most common types of scholarships is a merit-based scholarship. Merit-based scholarships are offered by your college based on your high school academic performance. This means that you'll receive more money from your college if you have a higher grade point average (GPA) or standardized test scores. Any merit-based scholarships that you qualify for will be determined when you submit your college application and are often included in your acceptance letter.

Other types of scholarships come from many different organizations, which means it's possible to get a scholarship for almost anything. You can get a scholarship for winning a robotics competition, writing the best poem, or even for community service. Check out as many scholarships as you can — you might be surprised by the types of things that qualify you for a scholarship.

TIPS FOR SAVING
MONEY IN COLLEGE

Even though college is expensive, you can still find ways to save without counting every penny. The best thing you can do is to keep track of your spending and stick to your budget. Let's take a look at some of the easiest ways to save money as a college student.

BUY USED
TEXTBOOKS

Unless the textbook itself is the newest edition and your professor requires that you use the newest edition, always buy used textbooks. While the "used" part of those cheaper textbooks may turn off some people, the textbooks themselves are almost always in good condition. Sure, there may be a bent page or some highlighting here and there, but you'll have all the content you need to be successful in class.

A second inexpensive alternative to buying brand-new textbooks is renting them. While there will be some textbooks that you may want to keep forever, such as books that pertain to your major, there will be others that you only need for one semester. You can save a lot of money if you choose to rent, and you won't have to figure out what to do with a stack of textbooks at the end of the semester.

Finally, another less expensive option is to buy virtual textbooks. These textbooks can be read on your laptop, phone, or tablet. Some people prefer to read actual books, but there are several advantages to using a virtual textbook. Not only do you have the ability to take notes as you read, but you can also highlight sections, look up words, and easily search for previous notes.

HAVE A ROOMMATE

During your first and sometimes second year of college, you'll be required to have a roommate. But after that, you'll have the option to stay on campus, move off campus with roommates, or get a place to yourself. While it may sound appealing to finally have a space of your own, it's also a lot more expensive. Instead of spending close to $1000 a month in most cities if you live alone, you could pay a quarter of that if you live with roommates. Not to mention that you'll probably have more fun and make more memories if you live with your college friends!

If you still feel you want your own space, you should consider being a Resident Assistant. This is the person who lives in the dorms as the supervisor for students who live there. They often are in charge of a hall or a floor and must always be available to the students who live there. Even though you would need to be on call 24/7 and may have to deal with some interesting situations, you could get free housing in return.

WORK DURING COLLEGE

Many students have one or more jobs during college, and this can be a great way to make some extra money and take out fewer loans. Yet, you do need to be careful how much you work. While money is important, so are your studies and your time for self-care and relaxing. You should make school a priority during college, but you also need to make sure to take time for yourself. Otherwise, you may not do as well in class as you'd like to, and you'll find yourself burning out.

BUDGET YOUR MONEY

It may seem obvious, but budgeting your money is harder than it seems. You can start by setting a goal for how much money you spend each month and do your best to stick to it. It may also help to determine how much money you want to spend on specific things, such as gas, food, and fun money. It's also a great idea to track how much money you spend each month. The good news is that there are so many apps that can help you do this!

ONLY TAKE OUT
LOANS YOU NEED

Generally, your loans will cover more than just your tuition—they can also cover your living expenses. You have the option to take out significantly more money than you actually need. Although you should absolutely take out enough money to cover necessities, try to avoid taking out excess amounts. Remember, you'll have to pay it all back once you're out in the real world.

CHAPTER THREE:

THE FIRST WEEK

The first week of college might be one of the most exciting weeks of your life, but it can also be a bit overwhelming and quite busy. It will be full of activities, events, orientations, your first classes, meeting a whole bunch of new people, and starting to learn how to navigate your way around campus. To help you avoid stress during your first week, let's walk through exactly what you can expect during welcome weekend and your first week of college.

WHAT IS WELCOME WEEKEND?

Even though every college does it a bit differently, your college will have a first weekend or week for freshmen to get used to their surroundings. During welcome weekend, you can participate in a host of activities and events that will help you familiarize yourself with the campus and make you excited about becoming part of the college community. You'll likely get a chance to settle into your dorm, meet your roommate and floormates, tour the campus, make sure you're registered for classes, and even attend some social events.

WHAT TO EXPECT DURING
YOUR FIRST WEEK ON CAMPUS

If you aren't excited for your first week at college, you probably will be after you get your feet wet. The first week is all about focusing on the incoming students—like you! This entire orientation week is dedicated to making sure you feel comfortable going to classes and getting started in your college career. So you can expect quite a bit of activity during this first week and weekend.

UPPERCLASSMEN
WON'T BE THERE

One thing to know about welcome weekend or welcome week is that upperclassmen won't be there at first. Although some colleges have freshmen move in one weekend before everyone else comes, other colleges may schedule an entire welcome week for freshmen before upperclassmen arrive. While campus may feel a little bit empty, use this time to get to know your surroundings without crowded hallways and masses of people.

THERE WILL BE
A LOT OF EVENTS

If there is one thing we know about welcome weekend, it's that it includes a full calendar! From social gatherings to dances to kickball, you can expect quite a bit from your welcome week events. Typically, there will be events for everyone so you can get to know people who have similar interests as you.

Make a point to go to the events that interest you so you can meet people and make friends. Or, you can step out of your comfort zone and try something new you may not have had the chance to do before. You might meet super cool people there and make connections that will last a lifetime.

HOW TO MAKE THE MOST
OUT OF YOUR FIRST WEEK

While it may be tempting to sit in your dorm room and prepare for your studies, it's definitely in your best interest to step out of your comfort zone and start trying new things so you can make the most of your first week.

Go to Welcome Week Events and Activities

The first thing you can do to make the most of your welcome weekend is to attend some events and activities. Although you don't need to go to every single event and every single activity, you should choose the ones you find most interesting so you can start to meet people with similar interests. If there's a movie night that sounds appealing, see if you can get people on your floor to go together, or if there's a field trip to a local hiking trail you want to check out, try to find people who are interested in that instead.

Find Your Classes

Another great thing to do during your first week or weekend is to find out ahead of time where your classes are. You don't want to be stumbling around, getting lost in the hallways as you're trying to make it to class on time, so find out where your rooms are or ask an upperclassman if they can help you find your way. That way, you'll be ready for your first week and feel more prepared for your classes.

Go to Student Resource Fairs

Student resource fairs have a ton of information that can absolutely help you be successful during your first semester of college. These fairs may have information about school meal plans, help you figure out where the nurse's office is, tell you about local jobs you could apply for, and give you general information about the town or your campus. These resource fairs are absolutely worth your time, so make sure you figure out when your welcome week fair is scheduled.

Explore Your Campus

Because you'll be super busy as soon as school gets started, spend some time this week figuring out where the best study spots are and determining where you want to do your schoolwork. While many students like to do their work in the library, see if your school has some outdoor spaces you can use to get some fresh air as you read your textbooks.

Get Organized

You won't want to be living out of boxes as you go into your first week of classes, so use part of your welcome week to get yourself organized. This means unpacking, organizing your school supplies, and starting to put things into your planner, so you know what's due when and to make sure you're prepared for the first semester. We will cover organization and time management later in this book, so read on for more to come.

Get to Know Your Floormates

Take some time during your first week to get to know the people around you, particularly the people you'll be living with. The people on your floor and in your hall are going to be your neighbors, so it's a good idea to get to know them, just in case you ever need a favor or a friendly face nearby. Positive relationships with others in your dorm can go a long way when making your first year a success!

Have Fun!

Above all, make sure to have some fun during your welcome week. College is stressful but will also be one of the most amazing experiences of your life. You're going to meet new people, experience new things, and put yourself out there in a way you've never done before. So, make sure you have fun during welcome week and make the most of it by going to events and activities, getting to know people, and spending the week getting ready for classes.

CHAPTER FOUR:

HOW TO PLAN YOUR COURSES

Even though it is commonly assumed that college will take four years to complete, it's often the case that it can take longer. Whether they need an extra semester or an extra year, students may be dismayed if they aren't able to graduate "on time." Even so, planning ahead can help you make sure that you graduate within those four years

WHAT IS A PART-TIME VS. FULL-TIME STUDENT?

As a college student, you have the option to either take classes as a part-time student or a full-time student. A full-time student is typically enrolled in at least twelve credits per semester, while a part-time student is enrolled in less than twelve credits per semester. So full-time students generally take at least four classes, whereas part-time students will only take two or three classes each semester.

That said, full-time students are set up to graduate within four years of starting their college program. While it does still happen that full-time students don't graduate on time for other reasons, part-time students will not graduate in four years and will likely need more time to complete their studies.

When you enroll in a college program, you'll typically be expected to be a full-time student, but that doesn't have to be the case. Some students find that being a part-time student works better for them because they're able to work or take care of family as they finish their college degree.

Even so, there are benefits to being a full-time student beyond finishing within those four years. Many schools will require part-time students to pay for each credit, whereas full-time students will reach a tuition cap after they take just four classes. This means that full-time students don't pay any more money for twelve credits than they would for eighteen credits. Some colleges do have extra fees for taking more than eighteen credits, but it really just depends on your school.

WHAT DOES IT MEAN TO HAVE PSEO AND COLLEGE CREDIT?

In high school, you may have had the opportunity to take either Post Secondary Enrollment Options (PSEO), Advanced Placement (AP) classes, or International Baccalaureate (IB) classes to receive college credit or to have the chance to pass a test to get college credit.

All of these classes are ways in which high school students have the opportunity to earn college credit. However, there is a key difference between PSEO classes and AP or IB classes. PSEO classes are college classes that serve as dual credits where high school students can get credit for both high school classes and college classes. AP and IB classes require students to take and pass a class, and they also need to achieve a certain score on an exam.

In addition, not all high schools offer every type of college credit opportunity. So if you're interested in taking college-level courses or getting college credit while you're still in high school, it's best to talk to your guidance counselor to see if your school offers any of these opportunities.

Earning credits in high school that could convert to credits for college is a great way to save money and make sure you graduate college on time. Because many high schools are public, you could essentially get college credit for free by taking those courses in high school. In addition, getting college credits this way often helps you get credit toward your general education requirements in college, so you can ideally spend less time in college. In fact, you could even graduate before the four years are up if you take enough college classes in high school.

Although AP credits are an excellent way to earn college credit ahead of time, keep in mind that not all colleges accept these credits. Further, some colleges require a specific score, such as a four out of five or higher, in order for it to count. That said if you plan to cash in AP credits as a way to knock off some college courses, make sure you apply to colleges that accept these credits and check what scores are required for the credits to count. In addition, you'll have to pay for your AP credit exam if you want to try for AP credit. The exams are usually not super expensive, but it's an expense you'll need to consider.

TIPS FOR STAYING ON TRACK TO GRADUATE IN FOUR YEARS

Making sure you graduate college in four years requires a lot of careful planning and effort on your part. You will need to consistently meet with your advisor and should be mindful of planning your classes and making sure you're giving your education your all.

Regular Meetings with Your Advisor

One of the best ways to stay on track to graduate on time is having regular meetings with your advisor. While you don't need to be in your advisor's office every week, it's a good idea to check in every month for a curriculum mapping and course meeting. Since your advisor will need to sign off on your classes, it's a good idea to meet with your advisor from the beginning and start developing a good relationship with them. Odds are you'll be coming back to them for a letter of reference down the line!

Refer to Your Major's Course Map

If you decide you want to study a specific major, that program will have a course map detailing the classes you'll need to take each semester or each year. Although some classes might be interchangeable, there are many classes you'll need to take as prerequisites for other classes. If you follow your course map carefully, you won't miss the classes that you need or forget to take a prerequisite. If you find yourself in this situation, it may delay your graduation because some classes are only available at certain times of the year.

Start with the Requirements

Especially if you're getting a liberal arts degree, it's important to start with the required classes. This means you should get your general education credits out of the way as early as you can, as well as working toward meeting your program's requirements. Once you have completed your major's requirements, you'll be able to take some fun classes as needed to reach the required 120 credits for a bachelor's degree.

Be a Full-Time Student

If you truly want to graduate on time, you need to be a full-time student. This means taking the maximum number of credits each semester, so you stay on track to reach 120 credits. If you're a part-time student or do not take your full credit hours, you may not have enough credits to graduate at the end of four years. You may have to stay for another semester or more to get your degree.

Take Only the Classes You Need

Although it may sound fun to take as many classes as you can in as many subjects as you can, this would be a waste of your time and your money. You'll need to take general education classes in different subjects, and you'll likely have some extra credits you can use for filler classes. However, make sure to take the classes you need before taking extra classes. Otherwise, you may not fulfill the requirements before graduation.

Pass Your Classes

This may seem obvious, but you need to pass your classes if you want to graduate on time. If you happen to fail a class, you'll have to retake it. If it is a major-specific class, you'll need to retake it in order to move on to more challenging required courses. So if you want to graduate in four years, make sure you study and give it your all. We'll offer tips on how to be a rock star student in the coming chapters, so keep reading to find out how to be the best student you can be.

Take Summer Classes

If you want to graduate in under four years or make up for failed classes, it's worth your time to take summer classes. The good news is that summer classes are typically shorter than classes offered in the fall and spring semesters, so they go by quickly. However, that also means you cover a semester's worth of material in a lot less time, so be prepared to work hard. In addition, scholarships and loans may not cover summer classes, so the expense may be out of pocket.

CHAPTER FIVE:

CHOOSING A MAJOR

What's your major? Odds are, this is the question you'll hear most often during your first year of college ad even in the years to follow. While it may seem like a simple question, it's not. Your major will influence your future career. So choosing your major is a big deal and is something you should consider carefully. But that doesn't mean that the process of choosing your major can't be fun too!

WHEN DO YOU NEED TO DECLARE YOUR MAJOR?

Although many incoming freshmen have a major declared before they even start their first semester, there are plenty of students who won't have a major selected yet. In fact, it's perfectly normal not to know what you want to do for the rest of your life at the young age of eighteen.

Typically, you'll be expected to declare your major by the end of your sophomore year. After your second year, you'll need to start taking more specialized classes, and if you haven't selected a major, you'll run out of general education courses to take. So spend some time during your freshman year figuring out what interests you so you can start thinking about what you want to major in.

ARE YOU ALLOWED TO CHANGE YOUR MAJOR?

Even if you start your first year of college with a specific major declared, you can always change your mind. Most students change their major, so it's perfectly normal to do so. After all, this is a big decision.

You don't have to start college with everything figured out in a tidy package. A big part of college is exploring your interests and trying new things to help you figure out what you want to do for the rest of your life. The best thing to do in the beginning is to take classes that interest you and figure out what you enjoy. It's also okay if you start with one major and then decide to completely change it up. Although it may mean that you'll need to take an extra semester or so to meet the requirements for your new major, the most important thing to consider is your future happiness and job satisfaction.

HOW TO CHOOSE
YOUR MAJOR

Every person's path to choosing a major and future career is different, so there are several things you can do to decide on the major that's right for you. Remember, your major is the first step in determining your future career, so think of an area of study that interests you and research jobs in that field to see if they might suit you.

Step 1: Brainstorm Your Passions and Interests

If you're truly stumped, start by making a list of all your passions and interests. In fact, it's helpful to create separate lists of your passions and your favorite activities to see if any of them overlap. Once you have a list of what you most enjoy doing, do some research to see if any of your interests align with a certain career path.

There are also quizzes and tests you can take online to match your interests, skills, and passions with career options. Although these may not be the most accurate (and you're certainly not committed to the results), taking these quizzes is a fun way to start thinking about majors that might suit you.

Step 2: List Your Strengths and Weaknesses

Another way to determine majors that might be a good fit for you is to make a list of your strengths and weaknesses. Now, this doesn't mean you should list everything you're good at and everything you're not good at — it simply means to start thinking about the skills you have and where they could best be applied.

For instance, not everyone is good at math. But if you are a math whiz, there are many different careers and majors you can explore that will use your math skills. You could go into engineering, statistics, or even become a math teacher. But if you're not good at math, these careers may not be a good fit. As another example, maybe you really enjoy art but don't want to be a traditional artist or teach art classes. Instead, you could look into graphic design or creating children's book illustrations. The opportunities are endless!

Step 3: Research Careers and Jobs that Align with Potential Majors

After you have identified some majors that could interest you, the next step is to start looking into the careers and jobs that you can go into with certain majors. Often, you can find lists of majors and common careers that align with them online or on your college's website. You could also talk to a career counselor or your advisor to see if they have any insights.

Your future career is even more important than your major, so see if you can brainstorm a list of jobs that you find interesting. Once you have some jobs in mind, see if you can interview someone who has a job in the career field that you're interested in. You could also find someone to shadow on the job or apply for a part-time job or internship in that field.

Step 4: Take Classes in that Major

The next step in determining your major is to take classes in that major to see what you think. It's easy to get excited about a major, but once you start taking classes in that area, you might find that it's not what you thought it was. So, the best way to see if a major fits your passions, interests, and goals is to take some related classes. You'll start by simply taking some introductory level classes or sitting in on some major-specific classes for upperclassmen to test the waters. Make sure you talk to students in that major, too—they can provide valuable insight.

Step 5: Declare Your Major

Finally, you're ready to declare your major. This occurs after you've researched various majors and careers and decided on the one that best fits your interests and goals. Declaring a major is easy—most of the time, you simply submit a signed document stating your major declaration. You may need to get an advisor's signature or talk to your student resources center, but the process is relatively simple.

USEFUL TIPS FOR CHOOSING YOUR MAJOR

If you're still stuck on choosing a major or worried about making such an important decision, there are several things you can do to make yourself more comfortable with your choice. But remember, you don't need to decide your major today — it's best to take your time to make sure you're making a choice you feel happy with. After all, this decision will impact your future and your career.

Take Classes in Different Subjects

If there are several majors you're interested in, take classes in different subjects to expose yourself to as many topics as possible. It's a good idea to take classes you know are interesting, but it's also beneficial to take classes that you wouldn't normally be interested in. This is where a liberal arts education can come in handy because you're required to take several general education credits before entering into major-specific classes. So try a few different subjects to see what you think. You might just find a new passion.

Pair Your Major with a Minor

If there are several majors you find interesting, there's always the option to choose two majors or pair your major with a minor. If the majors you're interested in are similar, there's a good chance the classes you need to take will overlap, and you might have the option to double major. If you're interested in pursuing a double major or a few minors, make sure you talk with your advisor to figure out the best steps for your curriculum plan. It just might mean that you need to take a few more classes each semester in order to graduate on time.

Choose a Major That Aligns with Your Career

If you want to be a dentist, it probably doesn't make too much sense to get a degree in marketing. Make sure you choose a major that aligns with your career goals. Although your major doesn't define your career, majoring in an area that aligns with your future career goals will likely help you get a job or internship after college.

Talk to Upperclassmen

Another good way to learn about your potential majors and decide if a particular major is right for you is to talk to upperclassmen. Juniors and seniors often serve as mentors for underclassmen in their college, so they are excellent resources to utilize if you're trying to decide what you want to study. Many of the upperclassmen have already gone through this major decision, so they can offer insights that could help you decide which major to pursue.

Talk to Professors

Professors are more than just teachers — they are your colleagues, and they are knowledgeable in their subjects. So if you're deciding on a major, it's definitely a good idea to talk to professors within that discipline. Your professors mentor students through these kinds of decisions all the time, and they can help set you on the right path to choosing the major that's right for you.

Determine How Much Education You Need

If you want to be a doctor, lawyer, psychologist, physical therapist, or occupational therapist, you'll need more than just a bachelor's degree. If you have a particular goal in mind for your career, you should research how much education you need to get into that field. Keep in mind that although many entry-level jobs require a bachelor's degree, many professions require additional education after your four-year degree. If you don't want to go on to grad school, it might be best to find a career that doesn't require more education.

Shadow if You Can

Finally, shadow if you can. Shadowing simply means that you follow or hang out with a professional who's already in the field to see what their job is like. So, if you're interested in becoming a physical therapist, contact a physical therapy clinic to see if you can come in to watch the physical therapists while they work. If you're interested in teaching, contact local schools to see if you can sit in on some of the classes. The best way to figure out if a career is right for you is to put yourself in that environment, and shadowing is an excellent way to do that.

CHAPTER SIX:

HOW TO MASTER TIME MANAGEMENT

It's 10:00 the night before a big test—your first midterm, in fact. You took some notes throughout the first half of the semester and figured you'd be fine for the test. But now that you've opened your notebook for the first time since taking your notes, you realize you're in trouble. You didn't know that so much content would be on one test, and now you're planning on an all-nighter just to have enough time to review everything.

One of the biggest mistakes you can make as a college student is waiting until the last minute to study, write a paper, or complete an assignment. Procrastinating is all too easy when you have class, social events, clubs, family obligations, and work. But pushing assignments off until the night they're due is a recipe for disaster, not to mention stressful.

So instead of submitting your assignments at 11:59 p.m. on the night they're due, make sure to stay organized, manage your time, and spread your assignments and studying out over time.

WHY IS TIME MANAGEMENT IMPORTANT?

If you have strong time management skills, you'll be able to complete more assignments in less time. By using your time efficiently, you can reduce stress, knock assignments off your to-do list, and have more time left over for fun activities, such as hanging out with friends or reading your favorite books. If you truly want the best college experience, you'll want to master time management.

THE DEVASTATING IMPACTS OF PROCRASTINATION

Procrastination just might be one of the most dangerous risks of college life. If you wait until the last minute to complete assignments, write papers, or study for tests, you'll be at risk for lower grades or even failing classes, not to mention higher levels of frustration, anxiety, stress, guilt, and more. When you wait too long to complete tasks and push off assignments for later, your workload will continue to grow until it becomes unmanageable. At that point, you may even begin to lapse on some of your assignments. The solution? Avoid procrastination with our tips in the following sections.

HOW TO MASTER TIME MANAGEMENT AS A COLLEGE STUDENT

Every student must find a way to manage assignments, study for exams, and write papers that works best for them. Don't be discouraged if it takes some trial and error to figure out a schedule that works for you. The best way to manage time is to keep a planner and stay organized, and the tips in the following sections will help you optimize your time, so everything gets done on or ahead of time.

Set Goals and Reasonable Deadlines

You won't be able to complete impossible goals or meet deadlines that are unreasonable. It's very important to make sure your goals are achievable in the time you set aside to complete them. For example, you might be setting yourself up for failure if you think you can write a ten-page research paper in two days. While we're not saying it's impossible, there's a good chance the paper won't be your best work, or it might not get done at all.

Instead, plan weekly goals for your paper, such as taking two weeks to gather research, two weeks to write, and one week to edit. By spreading the project over a sensible amount of time, you'll have a better chance to get it done and make sure it's perfect for submission. The same applies to studying for exams and completing projects. If you spread out your time logically, everything you turn in will be your best work, and you'll be a lot less stressed.

Identify Time Wasters

Time wasters can be anything that takes your attention away from the task you're trying to complete. Examples are your phone, video games, and even your friends. Many students try to multitask and study as they socialize or play video games, but this is almost never successful. Instead, find a quiet place to study and turn your phone off so you can be productive. You might even find that you have more time for the fun stuff later if you spend your study time wisely.

Use a Planner

A planner is a great tool for success in college. When you're taking multiple classes and have dozens of assignments due throughout a semester, it's easy to get lost, forget assignments, or fall behind on your work. Purchase a planner to help keep you and your assignments organized, so your schoolwork is finished by the due date.

Create a To-Do List and Stick to It!

Whether you make your list daily or weekly, creating a to-do list helps to keep you on track, so you know what assignments have to be completed in a given day or week. In fact, to-do lists are one of the best ways to set goals because you can list all the assignments you need to get done. The graphic below is one example of a to-do list that also allows you to prioritize your work. That way, you can complete urgent assignments first and move on to your less pressing tasks later. As you complete tasks, cross them off your to-do list. It's a great feeling to get things done!

Tackle Small Tasks First

Sometimes it's hard to get started with your homework because you have so many things to do. Instead of starting with a large assignment, try starting with the smaller, easier tasks. These tasks help you get into the study groove and motivate you to tackle larger projects. Plus, it feels super good to cross assignments off your list.

Break Large Tasks into Smaller Ones

Large papers, projects, and other assignments can seem daunting, which is why we often push them off until the last minute. Yet doing so may negatively impact your grade, especially if you don't get the assignment done or if you don't turn in your best work. Instead, try breaking down larger tasks into smaller tasks. That way, you can focus on completing smaller chunks of work instead of sitting down to do the entire project in one sitting.

Focus on One Assignment at a Time

Even though multitasking sounds appealing, it almost never ends well. If you're constantly going back and forth between assignments and never give one or the other your full attention, there's a good chance you won't be turning in your best work. Instead, focus on completing one task at a time. This doesn't mean you should sit down and write your entire term paper in one session. Focusing on one task at a time means taking one assignment or part of an assignment and completing it thoroughly before moving on to the next thing on your list. You'll feel more productive this way and will likely have a completed assignment to show for it.

Turn Off Your Phone

With constant dings and updates, keeping your phone on the desk as you do your homework will only distract you from your task. Even though it's tempting to keep your phone on while you work, you'll be much more productive if you turn it off and only have it out during your break.

Create a Routine

There is no better way to stay on task to complete assignments than to create a study routine that works. While some college students color-code their schedules and set aside specific hours to study each subject, it's just as helpful to set aside time each day to get work done. If you stick to your routine and learn to be productive during study hours, you won't need to cram at the end of the semester.

Schedule Your Breaks

No one expects you to sit for four hours straight and study the entire time. In fact, if you hold yourself to countless hours of straight studying, you're setting yourself up for failure. Instead, schedule study breaks every hour. Some students find it helpful to study for thirty minutes and then take a five-minute break, while others opt to work hard for an hour and then take a ten to fifteen-minute break. As you learn how to study, you'll find what works best for you, but make sure to give yourself a break!

Get Comfy, But Not Too Comfy

When you're ready to study, make sure you have a comfortable chair to sit on, and comfy clothes to wear that will help you relax for a productive study session. Some students love to study in the library, while others might prefer to take their books on a hike and read in a relaxing natural setting.

Just Do It

When you really don't want to complete an assignment, it's hard to muster the willpower to get it done. But because finishing homework is part of doing well in class, sometimes the best thing you can do is just sit down and do it! You'll feel better when it's finished, and then you can enjoy some free time.

Reward Yourself

If you're the type of person who likes to work toward a goal, then reward yourself for a job well done. Whether it's a tasty treat, watching an episode of your favorite show, or a trip to the bookstore, give yourself a reward when you finish a successful study session or complete a particularly difficult assignment.

CHAPTER SEVEN:

TIPS FOR ACHIEVING A 4.0

Even though college will be a ton of fun and games, your most important job as a student is to be successful in your classes and get good grades. Now, there's no one strategy that will help you pass all your classes, and it will take time for you to learn how you study and learn best. But there are several tips and tricks that can help you become a rock star student. So, follow these tips and create a plan to be successful in college and beyond.

WHY YOUR GPA MATTERS IN COLLEGE

Your grade point average, commonly known as GPA, is based on a scale from 0.0 to 4.0. This number indicates how well you're doing in your classes by compiling your grades for each class. Even though most of your grades appear as letter grades, they are converted based on this scale. Typically, a GPA between 1.0 and 2.0 indicates low performance, a GPA of 2.5 to 3.0 means you're doing well, and anything from 3.0 to 4.0 is excellent. You can also think of them as letter grades. Typically, 2.0 reflects a C average, 3.0 indicates a B average, and 4.0 comes out to an A average.

While it may seem like just a number, your GPA matters a lot. A good GPA means you will earn academic honors, and it can help you receive loans, scholarships, financial awards, and even jobs that will assist you in your career. In addition, many graduate programs require you to have a minimum GPA. If you have a lower GPA and want to get into grad school, you'll have to write an essay explaining your grades.

Your GPA also continues to matter after college. Even if you have no interest in going to graduate school, your GPA can still impact your future career. Typically, students with higher GPAs have a better likelihood of getting an internship after college and are better positioned to find that first job. If you have a good GPA, you can put it on your resume for future employers to see. Especially if you have no job experience, showing off a good GPA indicates that you have a good work ethic and work well under pressure. So, doing your best in your classes can greatly affect your future career.

HOW TO EXCEL IN YOUR CLASSES

Your GPA matters. But to have a good GPA you must do well in your classes and be a committed student. While this means you need to wake up when your alarm sounds so you can get to class, it also means you need to have a good study schedule and great organizational skills. For the best ways to do well in your classes, read on.

Attend All Your Classes

The only way to be successful in college is to go to class. If you don't go to class, you'll be missing out on crucial lecture information, exam tips, making friends in class, and establishing a connection with your professor. In addition, professors often notice the students who are always participating in class. You'll want to stand out as a student in order to get good recommendation letters from your professors, so you should make attending class a priority. Going to class is ultimately the most important thing you can do as a college student. If you do have to miss class, make it a rare occasion, and make sure you email your professor well ahead of time.

It's all too easy to wake up to your alarm clock, turn it off, roll over, and fall back asleep. But if you get into the bad habit of snoozing your alarm clock and skipping out on your 8:00 a.m. class, you'll have a hard time being successful in college. Unfortunately, first-year college students often have to take the earlier classes. That being the case, make sure you wake up on time regardless of your schedule.

If you're the type of person who finds it hard to get up in the morning, do your best to schedule afternoon classes whenever possible. Talk to your guidance counselor or advisor to plan the best possible schedule for your academic success. If your choices for class times are limited, you might be able to take some online courses if your school offers them.

Schedule Your Classes Throughout the Week

Even though it may be tempting to schedule all of your classes on the same day to get your classes over with, this can be a recipe for disaster. Remember, if your classes are all on the same day, it means that all your homework is going to be due at the same time too. Even with a good study schedule, you might sometimes find yourself waiting until the last minute to complete assignments because you have so much time in between your classes. You'll be kicking yourself if this happens often enough.

Additionally, attending all your classes on the same day is exhausting. It's important to pay attention in class and make sure you participate, so you don't want to be tired in class. Instead, you need to be attentive and alert enough to engage with your professor and the material. This will help you stand out as a star student.

When you intentionally spread your classes throughout the week, you'll be able to hold yourself accountable to study and do homework every day because you have a consistent routine. Further, scheduling your classes throughout the week gives you more time to complete assignments as they come on a steady basis without leaving too much time in between study sessions. Try to schedule your classes on Monday, Tuesday, Wednesday, and Thursday if you can. Some colleges have classes that meet Monday, Wednesday, and Friday, but there is also nothing wrong with giving yourself Friday off.

Set Planned Study Time

Instead of waiting until the last minute to study for your exams, set aside time each week to study for each class. Even if a class doesn't have any homework, spend some time going over the course material, so you're not cramming for your exams at the eleventh hour. If you spend a little bit of time reviewing lectures, homework, and labs, you'll be in a much better position to do well on your midterms and finals. Plus, many college classes have larger projects that are due at the end of the semester, so you can always get ahead on some of those more time-consuming tasks.

Be Present

You never want to fall asleep in the middle of class or doze off for too long. Not only will you miss important material, but you might also give your professor the wrong impression. Instead, always be attentive, make eye contact with your professor, ask questions, answer questions, and participate in all activities. This sets you above the other students in your class, and your professor will definitely notice.

Further, many professors now give out participation points in class which can bump up your grade at the end of the semester. But if you don't attend class and you don't participate in activities, you might lose those points, which can hurt you at the end of the semester. So instead of taking that hit to your grade, boost it by making sure to participate.

Read Your Textbooks Before Class

In college, you'll spend a significant amount of time reading your textbook. In fact, you can probably expect a couple of hours of reading per class each week in addition to your regular weekly assignments, projects, presentations, and papers. Reading is often the bane of college students' existence, but it's an incredibly important part of being successful in class.

If you read your textbook before attending class, you'll have a preview of the content your professor will cover before you even get to class. When you know what's coming, you'll be able to focus more on the content and less on having to take notes and learning new concepts. This lets you engage with what you're learning at a much higher level and increases the likelihood of learning in class.

There is a strategy to your academic reading. For some classes, you can likely get away with skimming the material or going through the textbook quickly. For others, it might help to determine the concepts you're familiar with, so you can dedicate more time to the ones you still need to learn. If there's a unit you already know something about, you can focus your study time on the things you haven't learned yet so you can be prepared for your exams.

Even so, some classes will require you to read the textbook more in depth. In fact, some of the professors take test questions or answers straight from the textbook. So if you don't read your book for class or exams, you might miss some information that could cause you to do poorly on a test.

Take Notes with a Strategy that Works for You

When you're sitting in class listening to your professor go over the material, always take notes. It's sometimes easy to fool ourselves into thinking that we'll remember something without writing it down when that's often not the case. So always come to class prepared to take notes in a notebook, on your laptop, or on the printout of presentation slides.

Some students find it useful to print the presentations ahead of time so they can review the class content and take notes on the presentation printout. This way, you won't have to write as many notes during class, which will save you precious time. Other students prefer to write their notes directly into a notebook or type them on their computer, so find a strategy that works for you. We recommend using a bunch of colorful pens, markers, and highlighters to make your notes look nice. When you take pride in your notes, they're often a lot better quality!

Participate in Class

Being present in class and actively listening is one thing, but participating in class is another. If you regularly ask questions, contribute to class discussions, and respectfully comment on your classmates' thoughts and opinions, you're bound to stand above the rest of the students in class. Even though some students prefer to sit in the back of the classroom, it's easier to participate if you sit close to the front, so keep that in mind.

Understand Your Learning Style

Understanding how you learn is critical to being a stellar college student. Some students find they learn best when they watch someone do something or when they look through maps, graphs, presentations, charts, or videos. Other students like to learn by interacting with the course material. Others learn best by listening to lectures, discussions, or audiobooks. Through trial and error, you'll figure out how you learn best, so use the method that suits your style.

Ask for Help

Asking for help is not a weakness—it's actually a sign of strength. You're never going to know everything or know how to do everything, so your best tactic for being a successful student is to always ask for help when you need it from professors, TAs, and classmates. Never be ashamed to ask for help—you'll likely learn the information you need, and it's also a great way to start making connections with the TAs and professors.

There are many resources you can use to get help. While some students like to go to their professors' designated office hours, other students go to TA help sessions, the writing center, tutor center, or they may set up group study sessions to go over the material with other students.

Study Groups

Planning study groups is a great way to learn your course material. When you review material with your classmates, they can help you see the information in a different way. In fact, that's one of the prime benefits of going to a study group. Other students may understand things differently than you do, and they may explain it in a way that's easier for you to understand. Plus, you might form great friendships with the people in your study group.

HOW TO SURVIVE
YOUR HARDEST CLASSES

There will be challenging classes. This is especially true as you get into your junior and senior years and you're taking specialized classes in your major. There may also be classes that make you rethink your decision to be a college student in the first place! However, don't give up. Remember that every student goes through challenging classes, and most survive unscathed. So even if there's a notorious "weed out" class that other students claim exists to turn students away from a specific major, follow the tips below to be as successful as possible in those tough classes.

Participate and Ask Questions

Even though participating and asking questions is important for any college class, it's especially important for difficult classes. Remember, you can receive participation points simply for engaging with the class material and being active in class discussions and projects. So if you're worried about your grade, showing up and participating is the best thing you can do.

If you don't understand something after class, always ask questions. Whether your question is to clarify what your professor said or have them explain a certain concept, never be afraid to speak up and ask for clarification. Odds are that other students in the class feel the same way and will appreciate you saying something.

Go to Class

We've said it before, and we'll say it again: if you want to be successful in college, go to class! Especially in harder classes, missing just one class session can put you far enough behind that catching up may become a struggle. College classes cover so much content in a short time that missing even one class can be the difference between getting an A or a B as a final grade. While this may seem a little extreme, it is the truth. So make it your goal to attend every class.

Go to Office Hours and Tutor Sessions

For more difficult classes, you might find yourself going to office hours or tutor sessions more frequently. Professors and TAs schedule these sessions so students can get the extra help they need to improve their grades. So, go to your professor's office hours when you need help and attend review sessions for maximum understanding and performance in your classes. You won't regret your commitment to learning. If you find yourself doing poorly at the end of the semester, but you have a track record of frequently attending review and tutor sessions, your professor will likely want to help you out.

Always Ask for Feedback

If you do poorly on an exam, project, or presentation, always ask for feedback from your professor. You can only improve if you know what to improve on, so working with your professor or TA to figure out how you can do better next time is a smart strategy. More likely than not, your professor or the TA will help you figure out a plan for doing better and help you understand concepts you might have missed before.

If you receive and incorporate feedback, your professor will know you're growing and trying, which may make them more lenient at the end of the semester if you need an extra boost.

CHAPTER EIGHT:

WORKING DURING COLLEGE

Many students work to pay for college as they attend classes. Working provides a bit of fun money and the freedom to occasionally get off campus. Some students just work part-time in college, while others take on up to thirty hours of work a week. If you're an adult student, you'll likely have other younger students working alongside you. Even new high school graduates take on jobs in college. It's a good idea to understand the pros and cons of working through college before you commit to working as a college student.

SHOULD YOU WORK DURING COLLEGE?

What students really need to consider before committing to jobs during college is how well they will be able to manage a busy lifestyle. A full-time college course load is similar to a full-time job, so adding more commitments to your week takes away from your study and extracurricular time. However, many students are successful working while they attend classes.

Consider the pros and cons of working while you're a student, as described in the sections below.

THE PROS OF WORKING DURING COLLEGE

There are many benefits to working through college. Not only will you make money, but you'll have a regular schedule to help you manage your time and dedicate productive study time. Further, you can gain professional experience and make great friends at your college job.

You'll Earn Money

One of the biggest and most obvious benefits of working in college is money. Life is expensive, and having a little extra spending money is great for going out to dinner with friends, buying new notebooks and pens, and living a comfortable lifestyle in general. In addition, you can use the money you make to pay for your tuition to enable you to take out fewer loans. Or, you can simply use your work money to pay for your food and housing, so you don't need to borrow money for living costs.

You'll Ace Time Management

If you work for twenty hours a week, attend classes for twenty hours a week, and spend ten to twenty hours a week studying, you'll be an ace at managing your time. Because you'll have fewer hours to do homework or study, you'll learn to be highly productive during your dedicated study time. You'll have such a tight schedule that you'll have to manage your time without having too much time in between. For some students, having too much free time encourages procrastination. If this sounds like you, you might be better off getting a job.

You'll Graduate with Less Debt

Along with making money, working your way through college can help you graduate with less debt. When students don't work, they have to take out money each semester to cover their living expenses — course credits, housing, food, gas, and more. These expenses add up quickly, so if you work, you might save yourself a lot of future debt. This is especially true if you take out loans that accrue interest while you're still a student because debt adds up quickly.

You'll Get Professional Experience

While money is a strong motivator in itself, gaining professional work experience in college might be even more important than cash. It's hard to get your first job when you don't have professional experience. Although some companies invest in training college students, most would prefer you to already have work experience. So if you can prove you have work experience that transfers to a future job, you'll be ahead of the crowd and may be more likely to get a job quickly after you graduate.

You'll Make New Friends

Sometimes you make your best friends at work. If you're a busy college student, it can be hard to set aside time to hang out with friends. For that reason, try to find a job that matches your interests so you can meet like-minded people to hang out with during work.

THE CONS OF WORKING DURING COLLEGE

While making money and having less debt probably sounds appealing, there are some negatives to working while in college. If you're not skilled at time management or stretch yourself too thin, working can negatively impact your study time and your grades. Make sure you take time to carefully consider the potential downfalls of working as a college student.

You'll Have Less Time to Study

The obvious drawback to working in college is that you will have less time to study, do your homework, and write your papers. Because you need to focus on your studies, having a job should only be a priority if you need the money to pay for classes or know you can manage the responsibility of being a student and working at the same time. Of course, many students need to work during college to make ends meet, but just know that there are many ways to have enough money during college that don't require you to stretch yourself thin.

You can always take out more loans if you need them or try to get a work-study job that works with your class schedule and perhaps lets you do homework on the job. If you're worried about not having enough time to study, look for a job that lets you read your textbook as you work.

You'll Have Less Free Time

It goes without saying that working in college limits your free time. While some students like to keep themselves busy, so they don't have downtime, others might find themselves burned out or drained if they try to do too much. So instead of jumping into a thirty-hour-a-week job as a first-year college student, see if you can start by working ten hours a week or less. That way, you can see just how much time you have and make sure there's enough time for your classes and your self-care too.

Trips Home Will Be Harder

Students don't always think about working weekends when they get a college job. If you have a job, you will likely need to work weekends, and this can make going home to visit family more difficult. If you attend college in another state, having to work weekends can limit your time to see your family to holidays only.

If you're the type of person who wants to go home to see your family and friends often, getting a job might limit your visits. If you don't mind seeing your family and friends less often, this might not impact you as much.

You Might Have to Work During Your Breaks

In addition to working weekends, having a college job could mean working during your winter, spring, and summer breaks. These breaks are meant to help you recover from the previous semester and prepare for the next one. But if you don't get a chance to relax during your breaks, you might find yourself burned out and have a difficult time returning as a successful student for the next semester.

While there are jobs that will let you work only during the school year, many off-campus jobs want you to be able to work year-round. However, work-study jobs are often scheduled only during the school year and can be a lot more flexible for students who want to go home during breaks. So, make sure you consider this possibility before you decide to find an off-campus job.

IN SUMMARY

Your decision to work during college is entirely your own. While some students need to work to help pay for college, other students might work to fill extra time. Keep in mind that many students work while in college, but that doesn't mean you have to. You can even spend your first year as a college student just getting used to your classes and the campus and then get a job later as you go into your remaining three years.

CHAPTER NINE:

STRESS MANAGEMENT

College is fun, but it can also be quite stressful. Not only are you living away from your parents for the first time, but you're also completely independent, have to get up on time in the morning all by yourself, manage your own money, and above all, do well in class. Alongside all of this, you'll need to take care of yourself and learn to manage your stress. If you're too stressed or feel overwhelmed, it's going to be hard to do well in your classes. So make sure to follow these stress management tips and take care of your mind and body.

HOW STRESS AFFECTS COLLEGE STUDENTS

Before we dive into common causes of stress and how to manage your stress, we should define what stress is and how it can affect you. Simply put, stress is your body's reaction to both positive and negative events that happen in your lifetime. There are two different kinds of stress — good and bad.

When you think of stress, you likely think of distress, which is a bad type of stress. This type of stress is usually caused by something negative that happens in your life, such as the loss of a loved one or the loss of a job. Eustress, on the other hand, is a positive type of stress that can motivate you to work harder or can be caused by positive events in your life, such as getting into college or making the varsity basketball team.

COMMON STRESS SYMPTOMS FOR COLLEGE STUDENTS

Stress comes in all shapes, sizes, and symptoms. While some people experience physical symptoms of stress, others may have emotional symptoms. Regardless, some common ways that stress can manifest include:

- **Physical symptoms**. Increased heart rate, fatigue, headaches, stomachaches, sweating, shortness of breath, and muscle tension.
- **Behavioral symptoms**. Poor sleeping habits, binge eating, reduced eating or spending less time with friends and family.
- **Emotional symptoms**. Being irritable, having increased worries, feeling helpless, feeling lonely, and experiencing rapid mood changes.
- **Cognitive symptoms**. Finding it difficult to concentrate, having a negative outlook on life, and even memory loss.

TYPICAL CAUSES OF STRESS
FOR COLLEGE STUDENTS

There are many stressors for college students. Not only do people experience stress differently, but different people have different thresholds for their stress. While some people find many situations stressful, others may only feel stressed during significant events. Some of the most common causes of stress for college students include:

- Feeling homesick
- Financial trouble
- Lack of close friends
- Living with strangers
- Living with roommates and dealing with conflict
- Coursework
- Exams
- Family problems
- Work schedules
- Unrealistic social obligations
- Romantic relationships
- Loss of a loved one
- Unrealistic family expectations

HOW TO MANAGE
STRESS IN COLLEGE

As a college student, there are many ways you can manage your stress. In fact, if you have a healthy lifestyle, you'll have a much easier time dealing with stress. There are some easy things that everyone can do to help manage stress in a way that doesn't take up too much time.

Eat Healthily

First, eat a healthy diet. This means choosing healthier foods from the lunchroom, perhaps choosing salad instead of pizza. Make an effort to eat nutritious meals with a good balance of carbohydrates, protein, fats, and nutrients.

Get Adequate Sleep

While it might be tempting to stay up all night and hang out with friends, you need to get enough sleep every night. As a student, you're balancing classes, work, and social obligations. It's all too easy to pull an all-nighter or stay up past midnight every night. Make sleep a priority and get at least eight hours every night if you want to feel your best and be able to handle your obligations, including stress.

Regular Exercise

Getting up and getting active is important to managing stress. When you're sedentary too long, your body begins to feel lethargic and tense. Instead, hit the gym three times a week or get outside for some mild exercise every day. A little bit is better than nothing, so push yourself to exercise regularly.

Don't Procrastinate

If you push everything off to the last minute, you're going to feel stressed. When midterms and finals come around, you'll have so much to do that if you're behind, you might never catch up. Instead of turning in your homework assignments at the last second, try to get things done ahead of time or work on your projects throughout the semester, so you don't end up feeling overwhelmed.

Create a Realistic Class and Study Schedule

While it's tempting to say you'll get all your homework done on Sunday and all your classes out of the way on Monday, this is not a realistic schedule and would cause you to procrastinate and burn out. Instead, schedule your classes and studying sessions evenly throughout the week so you can do your homework and assignments in small chunks. If you try to do everything at once, you might become overwhelmed and not get everything done.

Always Plan Time for Self-Care

Always set aside time to do things you enjoy. If you spend your entire college career hiding away studying, you're likely to burn out and be constantly stressed. Make sure to schedule time for important self-care activities.

GREAT SELF-CARE ACTIVITIES

When it comes to finding self-care activities, do the things you love. The best self-care activity is doing something you enjoy that also relaxes you. When you set aside time to take care of yourself, make sure to do something that helps you recharge and get ready to take on the week. Below are some of the best self-care activities for college students, but this is by no means an exhaustive list.

Exercise

Exercise releases endorphins, which help you feel happy and good about yourself. Not only is exercise good for your mind, but it's also good for your body. When you move your body, you release tension which allows you to relax and focus. The next time you're feeling tense or need a break, get in some exercise by riding a bike, jogging, or walking around your campus.

Meditation

Meditation is the act of blocking off outside distractions so that you can listen to your mind and body and open your thoughts to spiritual messages. Even though meditation is easier said than done, it's an excellent time to sit in a quiet location and just relax. There are many guided meditations you can find online or at a yoga class if you want to pair movement with mental relaxation time.

Get Outside to Walk or Hike

When you're inside studying all day, you might start to feel stuffed up. Some of the best self-care time is getting outside to walk, hike, or relax on the grass, soaking up some vitamin D. Sometimes, just getting some fresh air will help you feel better and ready to study. You can even mix up your study schedule by taking your textbook and a picnic blanket to enjoy the outdoors.

Get Off Campus

If you spend all your time studying on campus, you might start to feel a little cramped. In fact, some students find it better to get off campus to explore their college town during their free time. This can be as simple as finding a hiking trail, going downtown for brunch, or heading over to the best local coffee shop to take a breather. It's a great idea to get off campus and explore so you don't spend all your time studying.

Arts and Crafts

Sometimes getting out your paints, opening up a fresh pack of colored pencils, or grabbing yarn and a crochet hook is the best way to relax. If you're an artsy type and love to do crafts, use those skills for your self-care time. In addition, some colleges have arts and crafts clubs where you get together with friends and learn a new craft, so make sure to check out those options.

Hang Out with Friends

Some students hang out with friends as part of their self-care and recharge time. Don't spend your entire college experience shut up in your dorm room studying. Go socialize with your college friends and make some memories! Keep in mind, however, that not everyone finds social time relaxing. If you're an extrovert and love hanging out with people, then hanging with friends might be your go-to self-care choice. But if you're an introvert and need your me-time, try one of the other ideas mentioned here instead.

Watch Your Favorite Show or Play Your Favorite Video Game

As a college student, you might have very little time to watch television. Some students like to veg out in front of the TV and watch their favorite shows or play their favorite video games. If this sounds like your recharge time, put on your headphones and turn on your TV.

CHAPTER TEN:

HOW TO MANUEVER THE SOCIAL SCENE

One of the coolest things about college is that you'll meet people who come from very different backgrounds with diverse perspectives. When it comes to making friends in college, be intentional about meeting new people, yet try to let friendships happen naturally. Put yourself out there to meet new people, make an effort to introduce yourself, but let friendships develop without forcing them. Sometimes friendships are found in unexpected places, so be open to trying something new. You never know, you might just find your new best friend.

For some, the thought of meeting hundreds of new people is the most exciting thing ever. But for others, making friends can be stressful and overwhelming. It can be hard to cultivate deep relationships that lead to friendship when you're meeting new people every time you turn around. Here are several ways for you to not only meet new people but develop friendships that could last a lifetime.

WHERE TO FIND FRIENDS IN COLLEGE

It doesn't matter if you're a full-time student, part-time student, commuter student, transfer student, or online student; there are ways for you to find friends in college. The biggest and most important thing to do is go to events and put yourself out there. So, let's talk about the best places students can go to meet people at college.

Go to Campus Events

If you want to show college pride and also get to know other people in your school, go to campus events, including sports games, plays, musicals, art shows, and any other event happening on campus. If you go to campus events you find interesting; you'll likely meet people whose interests are similar to yours. If you really want to make new friends, make an appearance at these events.

Join Campus Organizations

Another great way to meet people is to join campus clubs, sports teams, and groups. Not only do colleges offer numerous campus organizations, but there are usually a diverse array of groups as well, so you can easily find something that interests you.

If you love to hike, love holding a paintbrush and canvas, or have an obsession with table tennis, you should absolutely see if your college offers clubs in your areas of interest. If you don't see a club you'd like to join, you can potentially create your own club. The opportunities are almost unlimited.

One of the best perks of joining a club or campus organization is the social scene. When you join a club, you'll be introduced to a whole group of people who share your interests. Your fellow club members could end up being close friends or at least a fun group to hang out with.

Talk to Your Classmates

One of the simplest things you can do to make friends in college is talk to everyone you come across. In fact, some colleges even recommend that you make it your goal to talk to at least one new person each day during the first semester of college. That way, you'll be exposed to a bunch of new people and can then start to develop deeper connections.

Be Friendly with Your Roommates and Floormates

Your roommate is going to be the person you share your space with for the next year, so it's in your best interest to get to know them. While you don't have to be best friends, your roommate might just be the person you become closest to in college.

Beyond your roommate, get to know the other people on your floor. It's a good idea to get to know as many floormates as possible in case you get locked out of your room. It rarely hurts to be friendly with your neighbors!

Join Informal Hangouts

If the people on your floor get together in a shared social space, join them! The best way to get to know people and make friends during your first year of college is to attend social events. Some of the best social scenes are the ones that happen spontaneously. So if you happen upon a group get-together, extend yourself and join game nights, movie nights, or campus events whenever you get the chance.

Join Online Social Groups

If you're a hybrid, online, or commuter student, joining online social groups can be a great way to get to know the people in your area. You can find these groups on social media websites, or you can make a social channel for some of your online classes where you and your classmates talk about everything and anything. If you feel comfortable, you can even suggest that your online group meet in person to do homework, work on projects, or do something unrelated to school.

Get Internships and Summer Research Positions

Your college fun doesn't have to stop when finals are over. Instead, see if you can get a summer internship or research position at your college. Not only are these amazing ways to gain experience for your future career, but they can also help you meet people in your major — people who have similar interests as you. Plus, working a summer gig is great for cultivating deeper relationships because there are fewer people on campus. You and your internship or research team will have plenty of opportunities to get to know each other.

Get a Job on or Off Campus

Getting a job on or off campus is a great way to meet new people. Because you work so closely with your team at work, they could become some of the closest friends you have in college. It's also great to make friends off campus so that you have multiple friend groups and a more diverse group of people to hang out with overall.

Do Your Homework in a Social Setting

Even though you sometimes need to find a secluded place to study, finding social settings to get homework done is a great way to make friends. Studying with your classmates can help you better understand tricky topics, not to mention it's a great way to work on group assignments. However, sometimes social homework sessions are not as productive as you'd like them to be. They are still a good way to bond with your classmates over schoolwork.

GENERAL TIPS FOR MAKING FRIENDS

If you're like many college students, the friends you had in high school have been your friends for most of your life. So the prospect of having to start over and make friends in college might seem intimidating. Follow these tips to help you make friends in your first year of college, and you're bound to make friendships that will last a lifetime.

Be Your Genuine Authentic Self

First and foremost, be yourself. Although college can be a time to start fresh, don't pretend to be something you're not. You want the friends you make in college to like you for who you really are and not for the person they think you are. Your new friends will appreciate your authenticity, and you'll be surprised by the positive response you get from friends who appreciate the real you. Always be your genuine, goofy, quirky self.

Put Yourself Out There During Orientation Week

During orientation week, no one knows anyone else yet. This is your opportunity to be as social as you can, to get a head start on getting to know new people. If you're prepared to introduce yourself to everyone, invite your new classmates to activities, and go out of your way to get to know the people in your dorm, you'll get noticed and start building connections.

However, this amount of socializing may not be something you're comfortable with, and that's okay. If you're shy, you can do as much or as little networking as you want. Even so, we encourage you to break out of your shell to meet new people and start developing friendships.

Introduce Yourself

You can't expect to make friends if you never introduce yourself or greet people in the hallway. So if you see someone you don't know, introduce yourself! During the first few months of college, everyone feels overwhelmed, and you can help others feel more comfortable by being friendly, taking the initiative to reach out to people, inviting people to activities, and even just waving to people in the hallways. You'll be surprised by how much everyone appreciates your efforts.

Take the Initiative to Invite People to Hang Out

You don't have to wait around to be invited out. Instead, take the initiative and be the one to make the plans. When a group of people is still getting to know each other, sometimes everyone stands around and wonders who will make the first move. If you gather everyone around and make plans, invite people to eat in the dining hall with you, invite your floormates to a study session, or make weekend plans to go for a hike, you're bound to start making friends quickly.

Talk to Someone New Each Day

If you're a competitive person or just trying to step out of your shell, challenge yourself to meet one new person every day during your first month in college. If you're at a large university, this task will be easier than you think. Even if you're at a smaller private school, you'll be surprised by how many people there are to meet.

Keep Your Dorm Room Door Open

Another great trick for making new friends during the first semester of college is to keep the door to your dorm room open when you're in the room. When your door is open, it's much more inviting for people to come in and talk or even just wave and say hi. Keeping your door open might even make your room the group hangout space, so you get to host all your friends.

Eat Your Breakfast, Lunch, and Dinner in the Dining Hall

Even though it's tempting to eat a granola bar in your dorm room or take a sandwich to go, one great thing you can do to start developing friendships is to eat all of your meals in the dining hall. Odds are you'll see someone familiar and will have someone to sit with. Because everyone is developing new friendships, eating in the dining hall is the perfect excuse to invite people to hang out with you.

Ask Questions

Introducing yourself is one thing, but really getting to know people is another. Focus on getting to know the people around you by asking questions about them. For instance, you can ask:

- Where are you from?
- Do you have brothers or sisters?
- Do you have pets?
- What do you like to do?
- What do you want to study?

- Do you play any sports?

Be an Active Listener

When you're talking to someone new, make sure you actively listen to the conversation. Not only will active listening help you learn more about the person you're talking to, but if you pay attention to the conversation, you'll be able to ask more specific questions. If you focus on learning more about that person, being a good listener will show that you're interested in what they have to say and getting to know them. Make sure you make eye contact, affirm that you're listening, face the person, keep your arms at your sides (not crossed), and always ask pertinent questions.

Befriend a Social Butterfly

If you're shy, one of the best ways for you to make friends in college is to become friends with a social butterfly. When you move in, you'll meet people who are clearly extroverts and love to get to know people. These are great people to hang out with because they will introduce you to new people, which will help you get out of your shell to reach outside your comfort zone and make new friends.

TIPS FOR MAKING FRIENDS
AS AN INTROVERT

A lot of people worry about being an introvert rather than being an extrovert. In college, you may feel pressure to act outgoing and more extroverted than you feel comfortable with. However, there is absolutely nothing wrong with being an introvert. In fact, the only difference between introverts and extroverts is how they like to relax.

Whereas extroverts feel more relaxed when they're around other people, introverts simply need to take alone time to recharge. Don't feel guilty if you need some time to yourself. If you're an introvert, here are some things that you can do to make new friends:

- Don't feel bad about making sure you have enough alone time.
- Find other introverts to hang out with.
- Focus on making one close friend or friend group.
- Get to know your roommate.
- Join clubs or groups that interest you.
- Don't overdo the social scene.

HOW TO MAKE FRIENDS
AS A COMMUTER

If you're commuting to your college classes, making friends can be a bit more difficult. Because most socializing happens in the dorms, many of the students living on campus will have a head start when it comes to meeting new friends. However, that doesn't mean you won't be able to make friends in college. It simply means you need to be more strategic in your effort to find them. For that reason, try some of the following tactics to make friends as a commuter student:

- Arrive at your classes early and stay late.
- Stay on campus for all your studying.
- Go to the dorms after hours, where a lot of activity occurs and where people make friendships.
- When you get invited somewhere, go!
- Invite people to hang out off campus.
- Join on-campus study groups.

HOW TO MAKE FRIENDS
AS A TRANSFER STUDENT

If you're in your second, third, or fourth year of college or transferring to a new college, making friends can be harder. However, many colleges have excellent transfer student programs to connect you with other transfer students or students who serve as mentors on campus. As a transfer student, here are some things you can do to make friends:

- Find other transfer students.
- Visit the transfer student organization.
- Study in group spaces on campus.
- Join clubs and groups.
- Find online communities for room and board and live with a roommate.
- Get to class early and stay late.

HOW TO MAKE FRIENDS AS AN ONLINE OR HYBRID STUDENT

More and more students are now taking online classes or taking a combination of online and in-person classes. While being an online student can be great for working during college or for saving money by living at home, it also means that it will be a little bit harder to make friends in college. Yet, there are still ways for you to make friends as an online or hybrid student, such as:

- Host online study groups.
- Host online social groups.

- Offer to meet other online students in person for study sessions or class projects.
- Go to campus to do your online classes.
- Find online groups or organizations to join.

  Get a job, volunteer, or get an internship.

CHAPTER ELEVEN:

MANAGING CONFLICT

When you live with other people, sharing space and getting used to new routines, conflict is inevitable. Even if your roommates are very similar to you, or you room with some of your best friends, there will still come a time when conflict occurs. Conflict doesn't have to be serious — it can sometimes be a buildup of many little things that just get on your nerves.

Instead of letting the little things build up, it's best to resolve conflict immediately and communicate openly with your roommates. But how do you solve conflict? Let's take a look at the best ways to resolve situations with your friends and roommates.

WHAT CAUSES CONFLICT WITH ROOMMATES?

Although conflict is sometimes caused by a specific event, other times, it can be the result of poor communication or just small annoyances that build up over time. In fact, most of the conflicts you'll come across will likely be caused by some sort of miscommunication. Other times, some of the following things might lead to conflict with your roommates:

- Staying out late and waking up your sleeping roommate when you return
- Staying up late playing loud video games
- Watching loud TV at night.
- Being noisy in the morning as you get ready
- Taking your roommates' things without permission
- Inviting people to your room without your roommates' permission
- Having different habits than your roommate
- Not keeping your living space clean and tidy

The good news is that most of these conflicts can be avoided if you openly communicate with your roommate and discuss your habits and expectations before move-in day. When you first find out who your roommate is, get together to talk about your pet peeves, living styles, and other expectations. That way, the two of you can figure out the best way to cohabitate.

TIPS FOR RESOLVING CONFLICT WITH FRIENDS AND ROOMMATES

When you're confronted with conflict, proceed carefully. Every situation is going to be different, so observe what's going on and decide the best course of action. The tips below will assist you when resolving conflicts with your roommates and friends.

Resolve Conflict Immediately, Don't Wait

First, never let conflict fester. Address the conflict or problem immediately, so it doesn't grow into something unresolvable. When you notice that something is off with your roommate, ask them what's wrong. If they're not upfront about what's bothering them, you should be clear and ask them if it's something you can help with or if they just need some space.

Or, if you notice that something you did bothered your roommate, talk about it. Never ignore your roommate's feelings. If they look uncomfortable, start by clearly stating what you noticed. Make sure you do this respectfully, so it doesn't come across the wrong way. Don't be confrontational, but state basic facts. For example, "I noticed that when I did _____, you seemed uncomfortable. Did I do something that bothered you?"

When Conflict Happens, Make Time for Honest Discussion

If something comes up between you and your roommate, make time to talk about it in person. If you don't, that one event might grow into something much larger that could compromise your friendship or your living situation. Pick a time that works for both of you to talk about it openly.

Evaluate Your Own Responses and Attitudes

Even though we'd like to always believe we didn't cause the problem, sometimes your own response to the situation or your own attitude can perpetuate the conflict. So when something does happen, make sure to evaluate the way you handled it and your attitude toward what happened. If you did or said something that made your roommate feel uncomfortable, you may need to admit that and work to change the behavior in the future.

Initiate Conversation About the Conflict

When conflict occurs, sometimes things happen that might make you or your roommate let out your emotions in unhealthy ways. If you don't take the time to actually discuss the conflict, someone may say or do something that makes things worse. Instead, make sure you initiate a conversation about the conflict to get everything out in the open. This honesty will help you to avoid gossip occurring behind someone's back and will make it much easier to find a satisfactory resolution.

Pick Your Battles Carefully

Sometimes, things happen that aren't worth battling over. For instance, if your roommate needs to have a fan on at night, even in the dead of winter, let them run the fan even if it means you need to use an extra blanket to stay warm. There are some things that aren't worth the argument, so pick your battles carefully and only confront your roommate about things that truly need to be discussed.

Learn to Agree to Disagree

You and your roommate will not agree on every single topic since every person is a unique individual with their own opinions, beliefs, and values. Chances are there will be times when you and your roommate disagree on something. Instead of trying to convince your roommate to agree with you, simply learn to agree to disagree and move on. If you value each other's differences, you'll have the opportunity to develop a much deeper friendship and relationship.

When All Else Fails, Get Help to Resolve Your Conflict

If you have tried everything you can to resolve conflict and you're still not getting anywhere, it might be time to get help. Luckily, this is where your RA comes in. Your RA is trained to help manage conflict with roommates so you two can come to a reasonable solution and continue living with each other for the rest of the year. There is a specific way to go about roommate mediation, which is discussed in the sections below.

HOW TO CONFRONT YOUR ROOMMATE TO RESOLVE CONFLICT

There's a right way and a wrong way to confront your roommate about a conflict. While some of this information may seem intuitive, not everyone knows how to approach their roommate when conflict occurs. The following tips will help you find the right time and place to discuss problems you've experienced with your friend or roommate.

Find the Right Time to Approach Your Roommate

The first step to approaching your roommate about conflict is finding the right time to talk about what happened. The right time is typically when the two of you are together in a private location with ample time to talk and when both of you are in the proper headspace to have a logical, calm conversation. For example, early morning, when you're rushing to get ready for class, is not the right time to talk to your roommate about a conflict.

Always Resolve Conflict in Person

While it may seem easier to text your roommate or leave a note explaining why you were bothered by something they did, that's not the right way to resolve conflict. Because text messages and notes are impersonal and can be misinterpreted, always have this conversation in person. When you talk to each other face to face, you can clearly listen to their side of the story and make sure you fully understand what happened so that you can both proceed appropriately.

Approach Your Roommate Privately

Don't approach your roommate about conflict when they're in a large group of people. This likely won't sit well with them and may cause a much bigger problem than you anticipated. Instead, always talk to your roommate in private or set aside a time for you to meet privately. If you approach your roommate in a public setting, it could be an unwelcome surprise or drama that could cause them to be defensive or embarrassed. When that happens, it could make the problem much larger than necessary.

Be Direct and Intentional in Your Approach

When you approach your roommate about conflict, be direct and intentional in your approach. Don't beat around the bush when you explain your situation. Further, make sure not to say something that would intentionally hurt your roommate. Instead, present the facts clearly, state what happened, and explain how it affected you. Practice what you want to say ahead of time. You could even run it by a trusted friend or your RA if you need feedback.

Listen to the Other Side of the Story

Because miscommunication and lack of communication can be a major source of conflict, listen to your roommate's side of the story before accusing them of something. The best way to approach your roommate about conflict is to state what happened and ask them how they perceived the situation to understand their perspective. After you hear their perspective, say how you felt so that both of you can come to an appropriate solution.

Be Willing to Compromise

When it comes to conflict, a solution may not be clear. Instead, both of you may need to compromise so you can reach a satisfactory resolution. While your roommate should be willing to compromise, you also need to be willing to compromise when you have that conversation.

HOW ROOMMATE MEDIATIONS WORK

When conflict gets out of hand, your RA may get involved as an unbiased third party. They can help you resolve the conflict or come up with a solution. RAs are trained in conflict resolution, so involving them is a smart move. You can generally expect the following from a roommate mediation:

- You can contact your RA via email or in person and explain the situation along with your request for mediation.
- Your RA will contact all roommates and find a time for everyone to meet in person.
- During the mediation, each person will have an uninterrupted chance to explain their side of the story.
- Your RA will go over your roommate contract to see how the two of you agreed to solve problems.
- Your RA may ask for possible ideas for solutions from each person.
- You'll be asked to come up with a compromise that you both feel comfortable with.
- Everyone involved will be asked to follow through on the compromise.
- If after the mediation there are still problems, you may need to repeat the mediation process.
- In extreme situations, one of the roommates may be assigned to another room/roommate.

CHAPTER TWELVE:

ESTABLISHING BALANCE

Time management is something all students have to learn if they want to balance their responsibilities in life. You're responsible for your student performance, and you also have friends, family, work, and other life responsibilities to fulfill. If you don't focus on balancing these responsibilities, you might find yourself burned out and overwhelmed.

By definition, work/life balance is essentially the way that people balance their work and play. Overworking yourself can lead to poor well-being with many negative impacts on your physical and mental health. There's no magic formula to creating a perfect work/life balance, but there are several ways to make sure you have enough time to satisfy all of your responsibilities.

The keys to maintaining school/life balance involve monitoring what you do while you're in school, but also what you do in your free time. If you enjoy your classes and also take the time to relax when you have the time, you'll find it much easier to balance all your responsibilities. Yet, this is often easier said than done, and many students struggle to balance schoolwork and other responsibilities.

SYMPTOMS OF BURNOUT

While everyone experiences burnout differently, there are common symptoms that many students experience. Feeling burnt out is more than just being tired. In fact, it can impact almost every area of your life, including personal relationships and academics. In addition, burnout may lead to the following:

- Feeling tired all the time
- Fatigue and insomnia
- Lack of motivation
- Poor class attendance and late assignments
- Feeling irritable or frustrated
- Lack of inspiration and creativity for projects
- Lack of confidence
- Inability to meet deadlines
- Headaches, sore muscles, or jaw tension
- Illness due to stress and exhaustion
- Overeating or undereating
- Difficulty concentrating
- Feeling disinterested or bored

BALANCING WORK
AND SCHOOL LIFE

Many college students find it difficult to manage their various responsibilities. You need to establish this balance if you want to be a successful college student without becoming overwhelmed. Your roles as student, employee, friend, family member, and partner may leave you conflicted and affect your school/life balance in every area of your life.

If you don't balance your work, school, and personal life, your academics can suffer. Being a student is a full-time job, but many students prioritize their academics at the expense of their personal relationships, health, exercise, and relaxation time. Not taking time to take care of yourself can result in burnout. This could lead to you not being able to do as well in your classes due to a lack of energy.

In addition, poor work/life balance negatively impacts your relationships. The quality of your relationships influences your ability to balance school life, but not having supportive relationships can also take a toll on your academics. For instance, if you have a fight with one of your best friends, it might be difficult to focus on your schoolwork. But if you put your schoolwork first and ignore the conflict, it could easily put a strain on the relationship.

The good news is there are ways for you to balance all your responsibilities, and you can achieve that by establishing a healthy school, work, and life balance.

HOW TO HAVE WORK/SCHOOL/LIFE BALANCE IN COLLEGE

Establishing a good work, school, and life balance while you're in college is easier said than done. However, there are many ways to work toward having a healthy balance of responsibilities and fun. Of course, every person's situation will be different, and some students will have more responsibilities to juggle than others. The tips below can help you avoid burnout and help you achieve balance in your college experience.

Maintain a Healthy Lifestyle

The first tip for creating a good balance between school and social life is to maintain a healthy lifestyle. If you get enough sleep, exercise, nutrition, and take care of yourself, you'll feel more ready to take on both schoolwork and employment. If you find yourself staying up too late, eating junk food, and sacrificing your workout time, you won't feel your best, and you'll be unable to give your responsibilities your all.

Remember You're Only Human

The next most important tip is remembering that you're only human. Too often, college students try to do too much and find themselves feeling overwhelmed with too many responsibilities. Especially during your first year of college, when you're getting used to classes, it can easily become a lot if you also join clubs, balance several friend groups, get a job, and are a student athlete. If you feel that you are juggling too much, reevaluate your responsibilities and see if you can let something go. There's no shame in admitting you've taken on too much and need to cut back.

Set Realistic Goals

In college, setting goals is one of the best ways to make sure you get your assignments done on time. However, goal setting is harder than it sounds. You need to know how long something will take, and you also need to balance that information with other priorities and deadlines.

For instance, that all-nighter might sound like a good idea, but you might not be able to get everything done in such a short amount of time. Or, it might seem easier to start a ten-page paper the morning of the day it's due because you know you'll be highly motivated, but you will probably not turn in your best work.

You may also err on the opposite side of the spectrum and set your goals too high. While you want to be as successful as possible, you also want to be realistic. For example, you may want to get all A's in college. Even though this is an excellent goal, keep in mind that you'll be balancing a lot and may find that your classes are much harder than they were in high school.

Master Time Management

Time management is a common theme in this book and with good reason. If you master time management, you'll be a great student, partner, friend, and employee. And if you manage your time well enough to get all your responsibilities out of the way, you'll have enough time to have fun and relax as well.

Prioritize

When you face several deadlines and have to choose what to work on, you'll need to prioritize. While it might seem like more fun to work on a project that isn't due for a couple of weeks instead of writing a boring case study due at the end of the current week, you need to prioritize your assignments in order of their due dates. It's all too easy to work on easy projects or fun assignments instead of difficult ones, but prioritizing will help you make sure that all of your school work gets done on time.

If you have a lot of school work and studying, and your friends invite you out to dinner, you might need to prioritize your school over your social life. While you need to make time for your friends and relaxation, your schoolwork has to come first.

Create Good Study Habits

If you create good study habits, follow a study schedule, and use your study sessions as productive time, you'll be able to get your work done. Even though most people have good intentions, sometimes study sessions are not as productive as you want them to be. So put your phone away and hit the books when it's time to do so—no excuses.

Learn How to Say No

For some people, learning to say no is incredibly difficult. If you're a people pleaser who likes to make everyone happy, you might find that you spread yourself too thin. In college, you have to learn how to establish healthy boundaries and figure out how much work is too much. Work on setting strong boundaries and learn to be okay with telling people no.

Go to Professors, TAs, and Classmates for Help

If you're feeling overwhelmed, you should absolutely ask for help. There are so many resources you can tap into as a college student; you're wasting resources if you don't take advantage of help from professors, TAs, and classmates. If you feel burned out or like you've taken on too much, use your resources so you can save yourself time and stress. Your professors are there to help you navigate your college experience, and they're there to help you better understand your academic subjects if you need extra help.

Focus on One Thing at a Time

When you have many things to do at once, it can be hard to focus on just one thing. But if you decide to multitask and work on several assignments at the same time to speed completion, you'll find that your efficiency suffers. Instead, prioritize your assignments and work on getting one project done at a time. If you need a break, give yourself a brief rest, and then come back to your assignment when you feel refreshed.

Create a Solid Support System

In college, you need your friend group and family members to help support you. By creating a solid support group of people who care about you, you'll have a better chance of being a successful student. Having just one person in your corner as an enthusiastic cheerleader can make all the difference. So, focus on making at least a friend or two for support (and be sure to reciprocate).

Set Aside Time for Fun

Last, make sure to set aside time for fun. If you focus your entire college experience on your academics, you'll likely start to burn out. Instead, make sure you set aside time each week to do the things that you enjoy. This special time is restorative and good for the soul. It's an important part of self-care.

WHAT TO DO WHEN YOU'RE BURNED OUT

Even with all the necessary precautions, sometimes burnout happens and comes seemingly out of nowhere. While, at times, you need to push yourself through feelings of stress, overwhelm, and exhaustion, there are some things you can do to combat burnout. As you consider the following ideas, take time to figure out what will work best for you.

Change Your Routine

Sometimes the best thing you can do for burnout is to change your routine. If you always study in your dorm room, try going to the lunchroom, the library, or outside on a picnic blanket. If you need to get off campus, try a local coffee shop, breakfast restaurant, bookstore, or park for a change of scenery. There are times when you're too distracted or too bored with your regular study routine, so reenergize your study schedule by going somewhere new.

Take a Break

Especially during midterms and finals, you might find yourself feeling burned out from all the studying. Even though you may have a strict study schedule with little time to waste, sometimes taking a break is the best thing you can do. Since you're no good if you can't focus, you'll need to set aside time to get away from your schoolwork. Then, go back to your studies once you're in a better headspace.

Evaluate How You Spend Your Time

Even though you may feel like you're studying around the clock or slaving away on projects for hours, some students are surprised at how inefficiently they spend their time. If you're the student who has their phone on the desk next to their textbook, constantly distracted by new notifications, you're not putting as much time into your schoolwork as you think you are. Put away your cellphone and turn off social media while you study.

Reach Out for Help

If you've given your all and you still feel burned out, there's absolutely nothing wrong with reaching out for help. Many college students struggle with establishing work/life balance, so there are resources available to you. Talk to your advisor, professors, or even the counseling center if you need extra tips for avoiding or working through burnout.

CHAPTER THIRTEEN:

WHAT TO KNOW ABOUT YOUR SENIOR YEAR

Even though this book has mostly focused on how to be successful during your first few years of college, there are some important things that you'll need to think about during your senior year. Some of the most important include: internships, job interviews, and grad school applications. Although it's never too early to start thinking about your future, senior year is the time to take action toward the next steps in your career.

YOUR MENTORS AND ADVISORS ARE YOUR GREATEST RESOURCES

Throughout your college years, remember that your mentors and advisors will be your greatest assets later in your college and career. You might need recommendation letters, and your advisors and mentors might also be able to help you get an internship or a job after graduating. Remember, networking is very important, and starting early to create that network for yourself can help you land jobs later.

THE GRAD SCHOOL CHECKLIST

If you're going off to grad school, there are some things that you'll need to have ready for your applications. Typically, you will start to apply to grad schools in the fall or winter of your senior year. Make sure you check the deadlines for the schools and programs you're interested in because they may differ depending on your discipline. Even so, you'll likely need the following for your grad school applications:

- Online application
- Official transcripts
- Two to three recommendation letters
- Standardized exam scores, such as the GRE
- Personal essays or personal statements
- Resume or CV

HOW TO PREPARE FOR THE WORKFORCE

Although you should be thinking about the jobs you might want to apply for throughout all four of your college years, there are some things that you'll especially need to think about during your senior year.

Get Your Documents in Order

Because you'll apply for jobs during your senior year and before you graduate from school, you want to have all of your documents ready to go for the applications. For instance, you'll need:

- Resume
- Cover letter
- LinkedIn profile
- Recommendation letters or references
- Work samples or portfolio

On-Campus Recruiting

During your senior year, look for job fairs or talk to recruiters who come to your school looking for new graduates who want to join their companies. You should absolutely set up meetings with them because they might be able to help you find a job.

Job Fairs

Your college might even have a specific job fair for juniors and seniors who are looking for internships or jobs after college. Job fairs are a great way to meet local business recruiters, and they can sometimes help you land an interview for a job after you graduate.

Internships

During college, try to get as many internships as you can. Although many internships happen during the summer, you can also take specific college classes that offer you credit for internships. If you're interested in internships, make sure you talk to your advisor to see if they know of opportunities in your area.

START THINKING ABOUT STUDENT LOANS

If you took out loans as a college student, you need to start thinking about repaying them after you graduate. Typically, students have a six-month grace period before they have to start making payments. Start thinking about paying back your loans during this grace period so you can get them paid them off quicker.

You may want to contact your loan provider to help with a payment plan that works best for you. You can choose from several different types of payment plans that work with your salary and can often shorten or extend the typical loan payment time.

HOW TO MAKE THE MOST OF YOUR SENIOR YEAR

Even though you have a lot to think about as a senior in college, you also want to make your last year special by having fun. You have likely met many amazing people along the way, so make sure you take the time to enjoy their company and continue to cultivate those relationships.

Get Involved in Student Life

As a senior student, all the students in your college start to look up to you. Get involved in student life by going to college events and activities such as sporting events, art fairs, and theater performances. A college is only as good as the students who attend, so show your student pride and enjoy all that your college has to offer.

Set Aside Time for Friends

Although you need to make sure you do well in your classes so you can graduate, it's also important to set aside time to be with your friends during your senior year. Because you'll all head your separate ways after college, make the most of the time you do have by getting together for study groups and after-school activities.

Schedule Reunions with College Friends

Along with setting aside time to hang out with your friends during senior year, you should also schedule reunions with your college friends. After you graduate, most college students don't get to spend as much time with their friends as they did during college. Some people will move away for their jobs or decide to move back to their hometown to be closer to family, so make sure you schedule some sort of trip where you can all meet up within a year after your graduation.

Have Fun!

Most importantly, remember to have fun during your senior year of college. This is potentially the last year you have to be a student. Even though some college students will go off to graduate school and further their education, this is the last time that many people will ever have to sit in a classroom. So, enjoy your last year of college so that you enter the workforce energized and ready to succeed in your future career.

CONCLUSION

Now that you've made it through this survival guide, you're ready to take on your college years and master everything that college entails, from being an excellent student to making friends that will last a lifetime to balancing all of your many responsibilities. While this book covers many topics, know that every single person's college experience is going to be different. However, if you follow the tips in this guide, you'll begin to develop the skills you need to be successful in college.

When you start college, you'll be thrown into an entirely new scene. This will be exciting and fun, but a lot of responsibilities come with your newfound freedom. While everything will seem new and fun at first, you might experience a brief time when you feel a bit down and perhaps homesick. Just know that these feelings will pass, and as you start to develop relationships with the people around you, you'll feel better.

The most important thing to do as a new college student is to make sure your needs are met. Listen to your body, mind, and soul so you can take good care of yourself. In addition, make sure you take time to have fun and enjoy your college years because they will be some of the best years of your life. Now, go on and have an absolutely amazing college experience!